SCHIRMER'S LIBRARY
OF MUSICAL CLASSICS

Vol. 1169

F. A. KUMMER

Violoncello Method

With an Appendix Containing
One Hundred and Eleven
Practice-Pieces

Revised and Fingered by

LEO SCHULZ

G. SCHIRMER, Inc.

DISTRIBUTED BY

HAL•LEONARD
CORPORATION
7777 W. BLUEMOUND RD. P.O. BOX 13819 MILWAUKEE, WI 53213

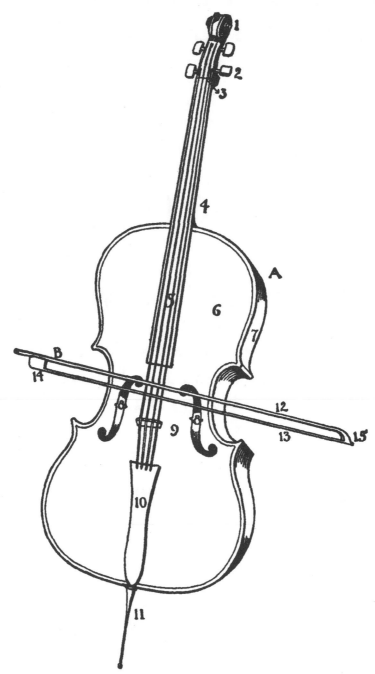

(A) THE INSTRUMENT·   1· THE SCROLL· 2· THE PEGS· 3· THE NUT·
                      4· THE NECK· 5· THE FINGER-BOARD· 6· THE BELLY·
                      7· THE SIDES· 8· THE F-HOLES· 9· THE BRIDGE·
                      10· THE TAIL-PIECE· 11· THE PROP·

(B) THE BOW·   12· THE STICK· 13· THE HAIR· 14· THE NUT·
                      15· THE POINT·

F. A. KUMMER ❧ VIOLONCELLO METHOD

PREFACE TO THE FIRST EDITION

After a considerable number of years, during which the author of the present work was engaged in tuition, he arrived at the conviction, that, notwithstanding the deserved reputation of many of the Violoncello-Schools already published, there is still room for an Instruction-book in which the closest attention should be given to the gradual increase in difficulty in the successive chapters, as well as to the accompanying examples for practical study.

If such a work cannot exactly be regarded as a necessity for those who, guided by the practical example of efficient teachers, enjoy advantages which can rarely or ever be offered by written explanations, yet it will appear all the more indispensable to the majority of students, whose circumstances admit of only scanty, or even inefficient, tuition. It is principally for this latter class of students that the author has attempted, in the present work, to supply the above-mentioned want, and to show, by simple and concise rules, the method which the student must follow closely when studying the Violoncello, without permitting himself any arbitrary abridgments or changes in the order of the chapters.

It is assumed that the student has already mastered the first rudiments of music in general; therefore, to avoid unnecessary details, the Introduction contains a mere explanation of the different clefs occurring in Violoncello-music; while in the book itself, everything is avoided which goes beyond the limits of instruction in Violoncello-playing.

The practical examples in the Appendix are to accompany the instructive chapters, as mentioned above; in each chapter reference is therefore made to the exercises belonging to it. For the better musical education of the pupil, and to render his task more agreeable, these exercises are accompanied by a second violoncello; and, although their number is greater here than in any similar work hitherto published, yet the resulting variety will doubtless be welcome to every student (particularly to amateurs), the object of these exercises being mainly to consolidate the pupil's technical knowledge on a firm basis, before passing to works of greater length and difficulty. After having studied them all, the following may be recommended for further development:

Dotzauer, 12 Exercises, Op. 47.	Merk, 20 Exercices, Op. 11.
Dotzauer, 12 Esercizi, Op. 70.	Duport, 21 Exercises.
Dotzauer, 24 Capricci, Op. 35.	Franchomme, 12 Caprices, Op. 7.
F. Grützmacher, Daily Exercises.	F. A. Kummer, 8 Grandes Etudes, Op. 44.

A. Piatti, Dodici Capricci, Op. 25.

Finally, let the pupil always remember that the highest aim of the virtuoso is, to combine perfect intonation, distinctness, taste and the greatest technical ability with the greatest volume of tone. In striving to attain these perfections he must never tire; and, even if in later years he should deserve to be classed among the Masters of the instrument, his artistic conscience will still tell him, that constant progress is necessary in art, because to remain stationary would be equivalent to the first step in a backward direction.

F. A. KUMMER.

PREFACE TO THE PRESENT EDITION

The technique of the Violoncello has recently undergone some changes, which the editor considered necessary to notice in order to put this School for the Violoncello on a thoroughly modern basis. The Exercises newly added are by Dotzauer [D.], Romberg [R.], or the editor [L. S.].

LEO SCHULZ.

CONTENTS

Introduction.

On the different Clefs.

The somewhat extended compass of the violoncello necessitates several clefs for convenience in reading the notes. The clef most in use is the Bass or F-clef, employed specially for the lower notes. It has the sign 𝄢. In this clef the notes on the lines are called 𝄢 *g b d f a*; those in the spaces 𝄢 *a c e g*; those above the staff 𝄢 *b c d e f g a*; those below the staff 𝄢 *f e d c*.

Besides the Bass Clef, the Tenor Clef 𝄡 is generally used for notes of medium pitch. In the Tenor Clef the notes on the lines are called 𝄡 *d f a c e*; those in the spaces 𝄡 *e g b d*; those above the staff 𝄡 *f g a b c*; those below it 𝄡 *c b a g*.

For the highest notes the Violin or Treble Clef 𝄞 is used. In this clef the notes on the lines are called 𝄞 *e g b d f*; those in the spaces 𝄞 *f a c e*; those above the staff 𝄞 *g a b c d e f g a*; those below it 𝄞 *d c b a g*. But observe, that composers were formerly in the habit of writing the notes in this clef an octave higher than they really sound. Therefore, all notes written in this clef in compositions by Mozart, Beethoven, etc., as well as in nearly all early works, must be played an octave lower. Even Onslow and several more recent masters employ this clef in the same way.

Finally, the Alto Clef 𝄡 sometimes occurs in violoncello-music. Although this is only very rarely the case, it may not be superfluous to mention it.* In this clef the notes on the lines are called 𝄡 *f a c e g*; those in the spaces 𝄡 *g b d f*; those above the lines 𝄡 *a b c d e f g*; below them 𝄡 *e d c*.

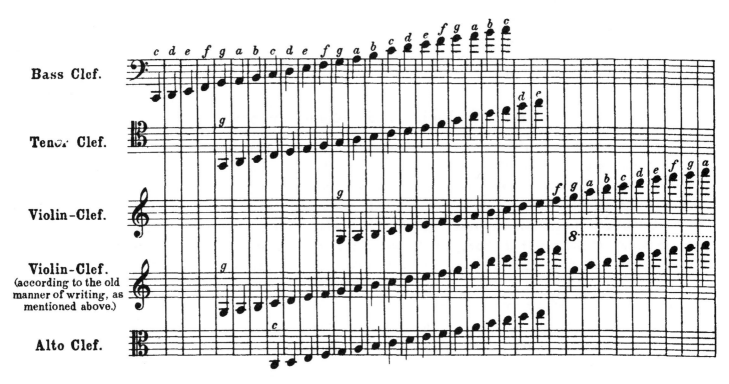

Bass Clef.

Tenor Clef.

Violin-Clef.

Violin-Clef.
(according to the old manner of writing, as mentioned above.)

Alto Clef.

* Boccherini very often employed the Alto Clef, Beethoven only once (in the 2nd movem. of the F-minor Quartet Nº 11); it also occurs in the works of Bach and Onslow. *L. S.*

15256 x   Printed in the U. S. A.

Violoncello - Method.

1. On holding the instrument.

The violoncello-player should sit well forward in the chair; his feet should be stretched forward, the left a little more than the right, while the upper part of the body remains in an erect and natural position. __ The instrument is held between and by the legs, so that the lower front edge on the right touches the right calf, and the left rear edge touches the left calf of the player. But avoid, as much as possible, covering the faces of the sides with the calves, as this interferes with the vibration of the instrument. The violoncello is held slightly inclined backward, and so far to the left, that the C-peg is about an inch from the player's face; the upper part of the back of the instrument will thus lean very gently against the chest of the player. The instrument should always be held so high, that the bow cannot strike the left knee. [This manner of holding the instrument is nearly obsolete; it is now usually supported below by a prop or standard, which should be long enough to raise the C-peg to the height of the left ear. But I consider it absolutely necessary, in order to learn to hold the instrument properly, to practise without any prop for the first year. *L. S.*]

2. Left hand.

The left hand holds the neck of the instrument in a curved form. The thumb lies on the back of the neck, opposite the forefinger and middle finger, and serves as a support to the whole hand. In order to produce a fine and full tone, the fingers should fall upon the strings like hammers, and press them down firmly with their tips; being kept, as a rule, so far apart, that they can easily execute the figure

without moving the hand in the least. __ The left elbow ought not to be raised too high.

The fingers are indicated by figures. 1 stands for the forefinger; 2 for the middle finger; 3 for the ring-finger; and 4 for the little finger. The sign for the thumb-position is ♀ or ȯ; the use of an open string is indicated by the sign ○.

3. Right hand. Guiding the bow.

The bow is held in the right hand between the thumb and the fingers. The thumb lies with its tip on the nut and the stick of the bow. Opposite lie the second and third fingers, in such a position that they also touch the lower edge of the nut. These three fingers, having to hold the bow, never shift their position; the first finger is held a little away from the others, and with the bend between the tip-joint and middle joint against the stick, in order to produce the pressure required in bowing. The little finger lies lightly on the stick, and preserves the equilibrium of the bow, *which must always be held without any stiffness in the wrist.* The tension of the bow should always be so adjusted that the stick remains slightly curved.

The bow should be drawn across the strings in a straight line, being always parallel with, and at a distance of about two inches from, the bridge. This is to be accomplished without any essential help from the upper arm, i. e., almost exclusively by the forearm alone; the motion of the arm should, therefore, be more from the elbow than from the shoulder. The elbow should always be held inward, towards the body, and ought never to be raised.

There are two different ways of bowing, viz:

      (1) the *down-bow* (from left to right) marked ⊓ (or ⋀) and

      (2) the *up-bow* (from right to left) marked V (or ⊔).

NB. The slur ⌒ signifies, that several notes in succession are to be played together in one bow; while dots placed above the notes signify that they are to be played short, one bow for each.

In the down-bow the nut is always inclined a little downwards; in the up-bow the *point* must be similarly inclined *). It is well to practise before a looking-glass at first, in order to observe more closely the manner of bowing and the position of the body.

Bow and wrist assume different positions according to the different strings. When playing on the C-string, the wrist is curved so far that all the hair lies quite flat on the string; for the G-string the wrist is a little less curved, and still less for the D-and A-strings.

The principal rule for bowing is, never to draw the bow harshly over the strings, either in *piano* or in *forte* passages.

   *) The pupil ought, at first, to draw the bow as straight and evenly as possible; for this undulatory bowing is apt to have disastrous results. [L. S.]

4. Tuning the Violoncello.

After the A-string, as the highest, has been tuned correctly, either with some instruments or according to the tuning-fork, the D-string is sounded together with it and tuned a fifth below A **). In tuning these two strings the fingers of the left hand, excepting the thumb, take hold of the corresponding pegs in such a way, that they can easily turn backwards or forwards as may be required. The thumb is placed on the opposite side of the scroll, in order to prevent, by counter pressure, the slipping-back of the peg. In tuning the G-and C-strings, the pegs are turned by the thumb and the 1st, 2nd and 3rd fingers, while the little finger manages the counter-pressure on the opposite side of the scroll.

A good and experienced ear is required in order to tune correctly; it might be of some help to the pupil to execute the figure upon the A-string, and then tune the D-string an octave lower than the last note. The same method will apply to the other strings.

   **) Take care that the bow does not engage one string more strongly than the other; otherwise the vibrations become unequal. [L. S.]

5. Preliminary Exercises.

Let the pupil remember what was said in Chapter 3 on *guiding the bow;* and, first of all, practise the following exercise, with the closest attention to bowing:

NB. Here the arm is extended at full length. Exercises for open strings will be found in the Appendix, a-e.

Then let him play the following little exercises, in which the left hand must remain steadily in the same position, without moving backwards or forwards.

6

Each of the following exercises must be practised very slowly to begin with; at first in whole notes, then in half notes, later in quarter notes.

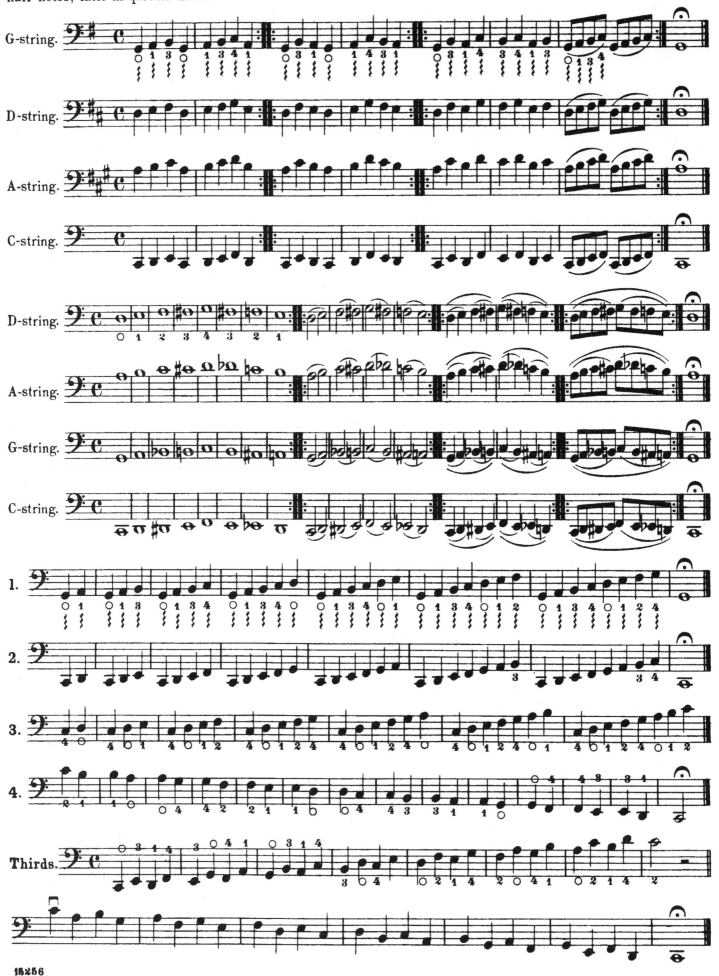

Numbers 1 to 5 of the Appendix are also preliminary exercises, and applicable here.

6. Scales.

The pupil will remember from his theoretical studies, that in music, 12 major scales have been adopted, each of which has a relative minor scale. They are distinguished both by their signatures and by their key-notes, as the following table shows:

Major Scales.

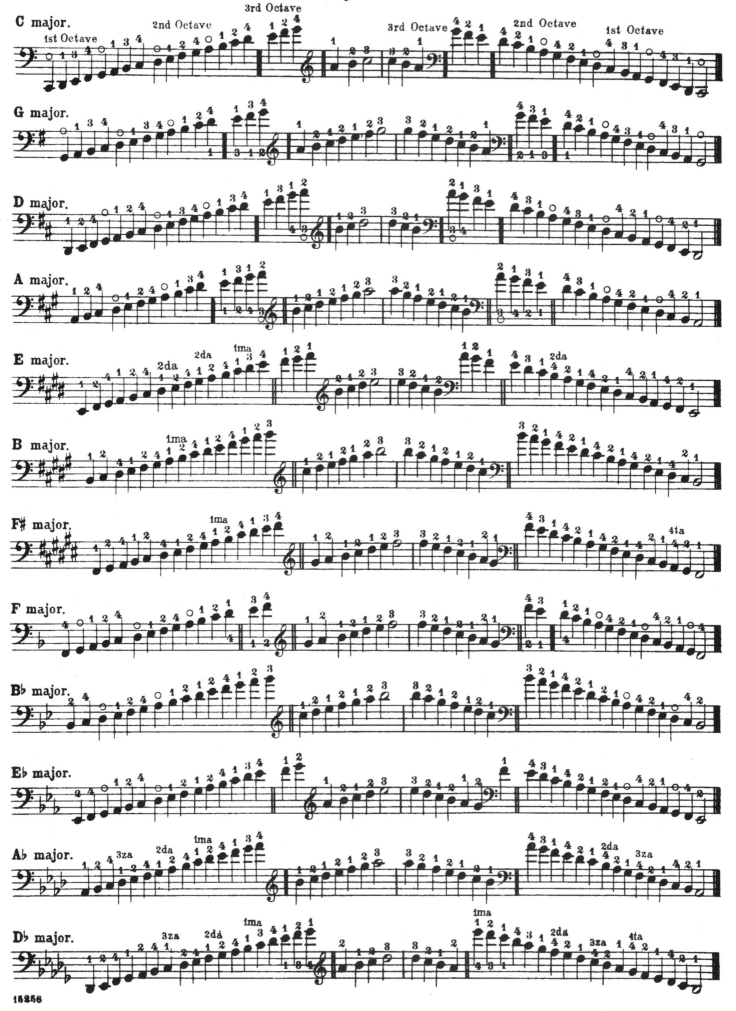

Minor Scales.

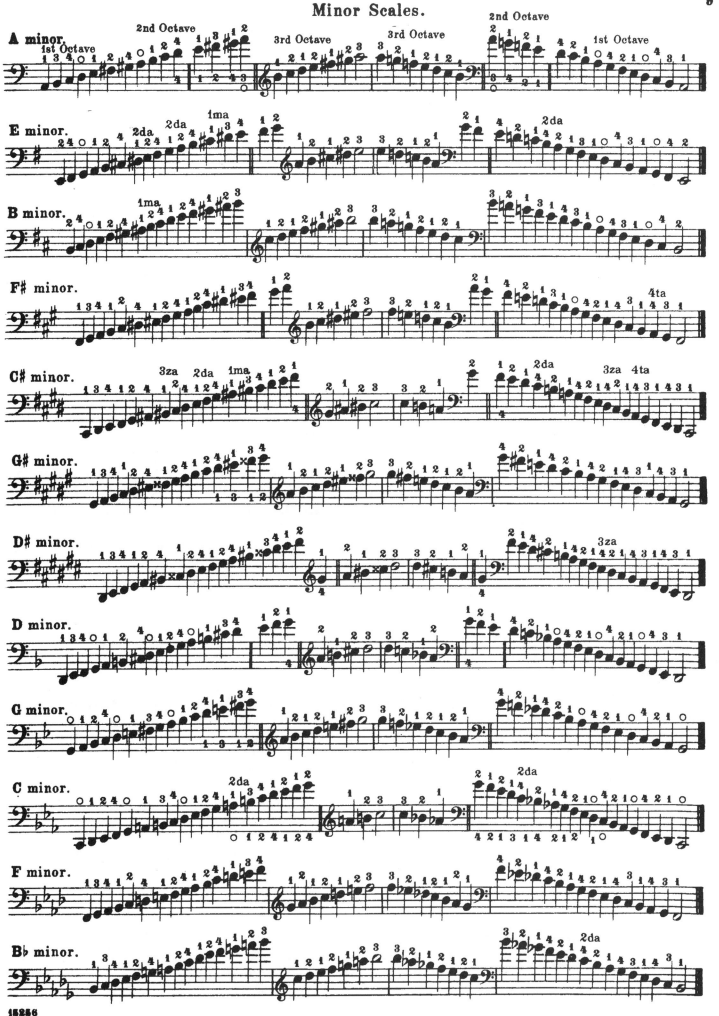

The major scales *C sharp* | *G sharp* | *G flat* | and *C flat* ‖ also *A sharp* | *E sharp* | *E flat* | and *A flat minor*
sound the same as *D flat* | *A flat* | *F sharp* | and *B major,* ‖ like *B flat* | *F nat'l.* | *D sharp* | and *G sharp minor*
their fingering is, therefore, the same.

By slowly progressing in the study of these scales, the student will infallibly acquire a thorough knowledge of the different keys, and may rely upon this study proving extremely useful to him with regard to pure intonation, tone, quickness of execution, ease of bowing etc. — For this purpose, however, he must

at first practise the scales of C, G, D, A, and F major, and A and D minor, up to  in the first position.

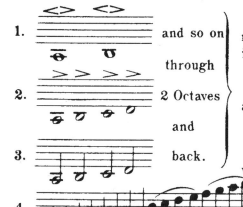

1. and so on

through

2. 2 Octaves

and

3. back.

1. The bow should be placed upon the strings gently, and close to the nut; as far as the middle of the bow the tone should increase gradually in strength, thence decreasing in the same manner.

2. Here the bow should begin with full tone, but without scratching, and diminish gradually.

3. The whole length of the bow should be drawn across the strings with equal strength, but softly.

4.

4. Here there are 4 quarter-notes to each bow. In the descending scale the notes from one string to another must be bound together with the greatest care, so that no break or harshness may be perceptible.

5.

6.

7.

8.

5. Here, too, in passing with the bow from one string to another, attention should be paid to smoothness and softness of tone.

6. These notes are played staccato, sharply and firmly, in the middle of the bow. In order to acquire strength at the upper part, they must also be practised at the point of the bow.

7. Here the first note is played with down-bow, and the remainder with up-bow.

8. These notes are played by lightly pushing the wrist, without moving the fore-arm.

On account of the dryness of scale-practice, it may be expecting too much from the pupil to insist on his thoroughly practising all the scales, before passing to the next chapters. After the scales in the first position have been thoroughly learned, all scales follow up to the 4th or 5th position, and in an order corresponding to that of the pieces given for practice in the Appendix. Further on, the scales must be practised up to three and four octaves (pp. 31, 32). Take care, in the higher positions, that the thumb follows all the motions of the hand, remaining a whole tone from the 1st finger in every position.

The *chromatic scale,* which consists only of semitones, can be played with various fingerings, and must be practised in several ways; yet the fingering above the notes is better than the two below.

Preliminary exercises in different keys are in the Appendix, Nos 8 to 18. The exercises in chromatic passages (Nos 86 and 87) are, however, to be attempted by the student only when he reaches them in regular order in the Appendix.

7. Fingering. Positions.

The preceding exercises, particularly the chromatic scale, have shown the pupil that, after making six stops in semitones on each of the lower strings, he reaches, with the seventh stop, the tone of the next string above. But in the following exercises and examples it will often occur, that

(1) to retain the left hand in as quiet a position as possible, and
(2) to be able to produce double-stops,

one is obliged to go up so high with the left hand, not only on the A-string, but also on the three others, that the above-mentioned 6 stops are considerably overstepped. —

In this case, whatever is to be played

on the A-string is marked 1ᵐᵃ which stands for *prima corda,* first string,
D „ „ „ 2ᵈᵃ „ „ „ *seconda* „ second „
G „ „ „ 3ᶻᵃ „ „ „ *terza* „ third „
C „ „ „ 4ᵗᵃ „ „ „ *quarta* „ fourth „

By this moving upwards of the left hand we pass through a number of what are called *positions* of the same. We may consider the two principal positions to be the following:

a) when the hand is so placed on the neck of the instrument, that by setting the 1ˢᵗ finger upon the A-string the note *b* is produced (1st Position), and b) when it lies higher up, the same finger on the same string producing the note *e* (4th Position). To reach the 4th Position readily, carry the thumb down the neck as far as it can go. Then, holding the hand free, one can take *e*, 4th position, with the forefinger. The other positions, lying below, between and above these two principal ones, are shown in the following table; the more difficult ones, which require considerable stretching of the fingers, are marked thus: ⌇⌇⌇

It will be observed that if, in the 1ˢᵗ position on any string, three whole tones occur in succession, they are always played with the 1ˢᵗ, 2ⁿᵈ and 4ᵗʰ fingers; for instance:

Studies for Practice.

Each of these exercises, like all the following, be repeated until the fingers have perfectly mastered the different figures. Although it is not indispensable, yet it will be found very advantageous, to let the finger taking the notes marked (○) remain on them as long as possible. Practise these finger-exercises at first on the D-string, then on the A- and G-strings.

Exercises for fingering in all positions will be found in the Appendix, № 19 to 42.

8. The Right Wrist.

The wrist must always be carefully watched by the violoncello-player, as all changes of the bow must be executed solely by it, without moving the upper arm. In order to acquire this accomplishment, let the pupil diligently study the following examples, and let him prevent, while studying them, any motion of the right upper arm by leaning it against a table or cupboard.

Exercises for the Right Wrist.

To be played in the middle of the bow.

NB. To enable the pupil also to practise these examples on the A-and D-strings, let him imagine them to be in the tenor clef with two sharps  and a ♮ instead of each of the ♭ occurring in examples 3 and 4; in No 5 a ♯ instead of the ♮.

Other exercises for the wrist will be found in the Appendix, Nos. 43 to 51.

9. The different Bowings.

The different bowing result from the ever-varying combinations of slurred and detached notes in down-bows and up-bows, and have an important influence on the whole character of the pieces to be performed. Composers are, therefore, in the habit of distinctly marking passages which require a certain accent by the style of bowing in which they are played; the following examples will demonstrate this.— But where these distinct marks are wanting, the pupil should make it a rule, to divide and arrange the different bowings so that, wherever possible, the first note of each measure be played with a down-bow. For this reason, whenever a piece of music begins with a partial measure, the up-bow is used in the beginning; for instance:

Of course, this rule has innumerable exceptions in the middle of pieces of music; because, to apply it universally, each measure would have to contain an even number of notes; but in most cases it should be adhered to, and it would be decidedly wrong, if one measure should happen to begin with an up-bow, were the player to continue this contrary mode of bowing for several following measures.

In this case it is better, at some convenient place, e. g; at a short rest or pause, to repeat the up-bow or down-bow in order to resume the regular mode of bowing.

N. B. Of course, figures often occur, progressing through a long series of measures, which can be played with ease only with an up-bow; for instance Nos. 1, 2, 5, 6, 7, 14 and 15 of the exercises in the last chapter; these are some of the exceptions above mentioned.

On the different Bowings.

The following example, which consists of a uniform number of quavers in succession will serve to make the pupil better acquainted with the different bowings.

It will be necessary for him to practise it carefully and slowly, in each of the various manners indicated, as only in this way will he be able to acquire the requisite freedom and ease in the guidance of the bow. —

N. B. In each of the following variations in the manner of bowing, we give only the first measure of the above exercise, in order to save space.

a Slurred notes (legato.)

When playing legato, the bow must always be placed upon the strings gently, and drawn across them with uniform strength in a straight line, without moving nearer to or further from the bridge.

1. Two eighth-notes to each bow, to be played in the middle of the bow.

2. Four eighth-notes to each bow. Here nearly the whole length of the bow is used.

3. In this legato of eighth-notes, the bow is placed upon the string quite close to the nut, and drawn to the very point; in the second measure in the up-bow, the reverse of course takes place. No part of the bow is to be left unused, and all notes must be quite equal in strength and duration.

4. 5. The four slurred notes are played with nearly the whole bow; the other groups of only two slurred notes are played at the point in No 4, and at the nut in No 5. The second measure begins with an up-bow, in both examples.

6. 7. 8. Here the short legatos must be executed with the same length of bow as the longer ones.

9. These are played in the middle of the bow.

b Legato and detached (staccato) notes mixed.

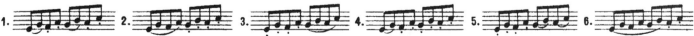

The legato notes here require a long bow, while the others, marked with dots, are played shortly and firmly either at the point or at the nut.

Here the single detached note must be played with the same length of bow as the legato notes together.

11. 12. 13. 14. These notes are played in the middle of the bow.

C. Dotted notes.

1. Here two notes are played in one bow; the first one rather long, while the second, shorter one, is to be played sharply and staccato.

2. 3. Here the second (short) note requires the same length of bow as the first one.

Examples for the application of these different ways of bowing are found in the Appendix (Nos. 52 to 71).

10. The Arpeggio.

The arpeggio is a broken chord, which is executed on 3 or 4 strings with a sort of undulating motion in the **bowing,** as the chord rises and falls. It is particularly brilliant and effective upon the violoncello, of all stringed instruments; the pupil will not find it difficult, if he has previously well practised the exercises for the right wrist **(page 13).** In the Arpeggio, as in the exercises referred to, all changes of the bow, and its passing from one string to another, are accomplished by the wrist, and the latter is to be aided only slightly by a corresponding motion of the fore-arm. One must not raise the upper arm too much.

The Arpeggio requires about two-thirds of the length of the bow. The lowest note must always be accentuated a little; the fingers must fall on the strings as simultaneously as possible, and remain on them wherever practicable.

Exercises on the arpeggio.
Arpeggio upon 3 strings.

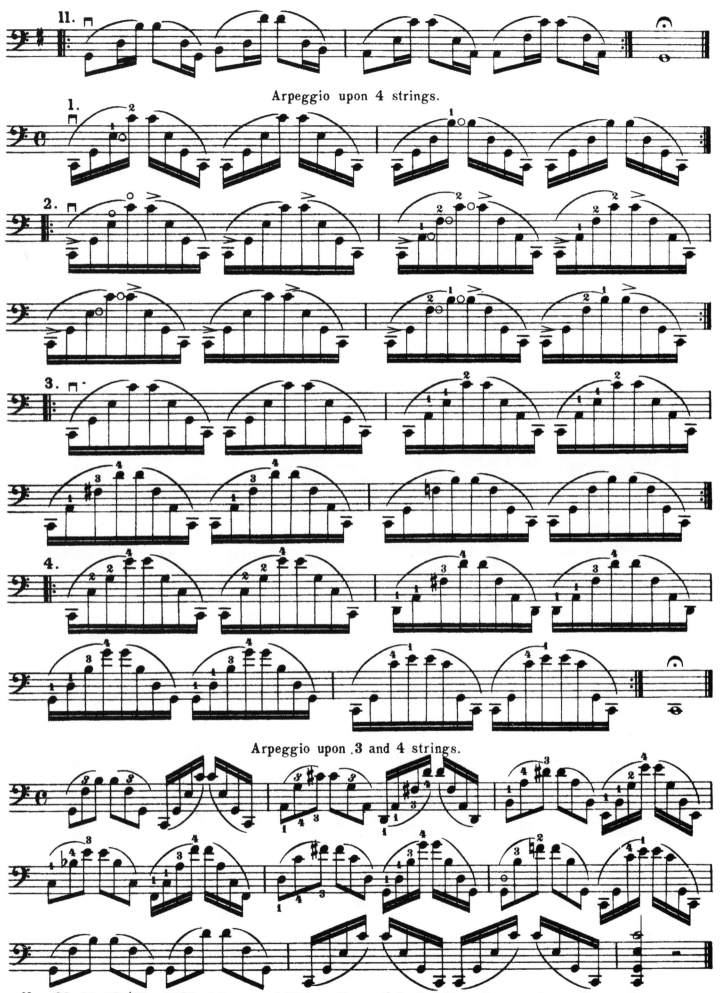

Arpeggio upon 4 strings.

Arpeggio upon 3 and 4 strings.

Nos. 88, 89, 90 (75 and 108 of the second Violoncello-part) in the Appendix, are Arpeggio-exercises.

15256

11. The Staccato.

By *Staccato* we mean the playing of several detached notes in one bow.

A good staccato is a natural gift of some players; but is also within the reach of others less favored by nature. From one to two hours of daily staccato-practice are necessary. The preliminary studies which I have added must not be practised with the wrist.

Preliminary Studies.

In the next exercises, after the first note, which is to be played with a down-bow drawn out to the very point, the right hand moves the bow along sharply and firmly in the up-bow, without lifting it from the strings, and uses as little of the bow as possible for each note. In doing this, the forefinger of the right hand presses a little harder than usual upon the stick. The first and last notes must always be accentuated a little.

Exercises on the Staccato.

Sometimes a *Staccato* occurs which is mixed with legato notes; this must also be executed in one bow, for instance:

In Nos. 91 and 92 of the Appendix, in the former number in both parts, there are exercises for the Staccato.

12. Graces.

The Appoggiatura, Turn, Passing Trill and Trill.

Of the great number of musical graces we mention only those chiefly in use, and explain the signs which have been adopted for them. Composers generally write out most of the others in small notes.

(1) The *Appoggiatura* may be long or short, and consists of *one* or *more* notes (double appoggiatura). The long appoggiatura occupies one-half the time-value of the principal note, if this principal note can be divided into two equal parts. But if the principal note is *tripartite* instead of bipartite, the appoggiatura occupies two-thirds of its value; for instance:

The short appoggiatura, whether consisting of one or of more notes, is quickly slurred into the principal note; for instance:

As a rule, the short **appoggiaturas** (consisting of only one note) are marked, to distinguish them from the long ones, with a stroke across the hook of the note; thus:  etc.

(2) The *Turn,* indicated by the sign ∾, requires both the next upper and lower notes, as auxiliaries to the principal note, for execution (ex. 1, 2, 3 and 6); the *back turn* (sign ∾; examples 4 and 5) is now generally written out in full:

If either of these auxiliary notes is to be raised or lowered, a ♯, ♭, or ♮ is placed above or below the sign ∾; above, it applies to the upper, below, to the lower auxiliary note; for instance:

(3) The *Passing Trill,* marked ∿, must be executed very quickly and roundly, as follows:

(4) The *Trill* (𝆖) consists in the rapid alternation of two notes; namely the one over which the sign 𝆖 stands, and the next note above it in the key in which the piece is written. The interval may, therefore, be a semitone or a whole tone. As a rule, each trill must have *an afterbeat,* which is formed by the note next below the principal note and the principal note itself. The trill is also often prepared by the note next below the principal note.

Practise the Trill slowly at first, so that it may become perfectly clear and even.

In the following example several kinds of trills are shown:

In a series (or chain) of trills the afterbeat is omitted in every one but the last of the series; for instance:

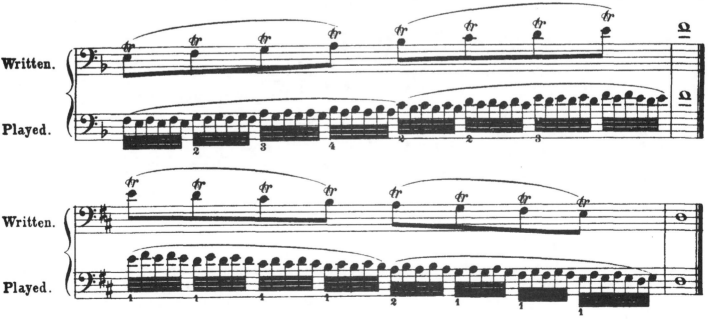

If the trill is made on a note lengthened in value by a dot, the following short note very often forms the termination; for instance:

Exercises on the Trill.

Exercises on the above-mentioned trills will be found in the Appendix, Nos. 93 to 98 inclusive.

13. Double-stops.

In playing double-stops, the bow must engage two strings at once, firmly and evenly. The student must bestow the greatest attention upon perfect intonation, and should practise the following examples (preliminary to Nos. 99, 100, 101 of the Appendix) slowly at first, with strictest care that not the least imperfection in intonation escapes his ear. The fingers must be set upon the strings simultaneously, and very firmly.

Exerercises in double-stops.

Scale of D major with thirds above.

Scale of A major with sixths below.

E minor.　　　　F major.

B♭ major.　　　　C minor.

Trills in double-stops.

Double Trills.

14. The Thumb-position.

This is one of the most important manipulations in violoncello-playing; for without it innumerable passages would be impossible. The thumb of the left hand is placed upon two strings at the same time (forming a second nut), raising their pitch to any desired height, and materially assisting the other fingers. It presses the strings with the outer edge of its upper joint, and in such a position, that the lower string lies nearly opposite the middle of the nail, and the higher one close to the joint of the thumb. It must be placed horizontally and pressed down firmly, so that the notes produced form a perfect fifth; this is, of course, possible only when the open strings are accurately tuned.

Take good care while playing that the fingers do not bend inward, but curve slightly outward and fall straight on the strings. At first the thumb will feel a trifle sore, but this does no harm and will gradually cease after further practice. To make the fingers quite independent of the thumb, it is a good plan to practise the scales without the bow, employing the right hand to aid the left thumb in pressing firmly on the strings.

Scales in the thumb-position (must also be practised legato).

The fingering for all the other scales is the same.

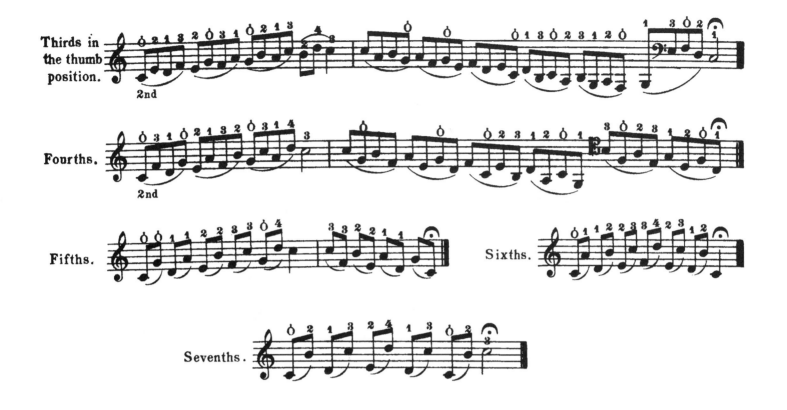

Thirds in the thumb position.

Fourths.

Fifths.

Sixths.

Sevenths.

Chromatic scales in the thumb-position.

C major.

D major.

Exercises for the fourth finger in the thumb-position.

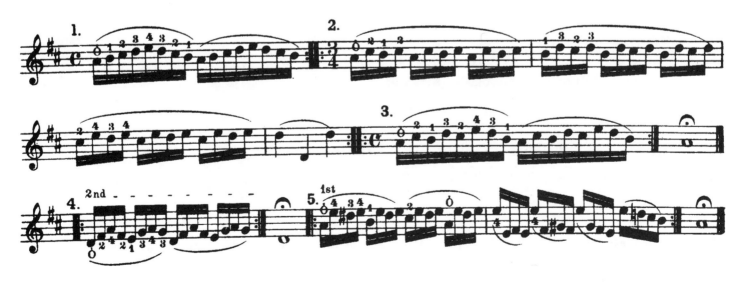

Exercises in moving the thumb along in the thumb-position.

Practise all these legato with long bows, and also staccato in the middle of the bow.

Scales with prepared thumb-position.

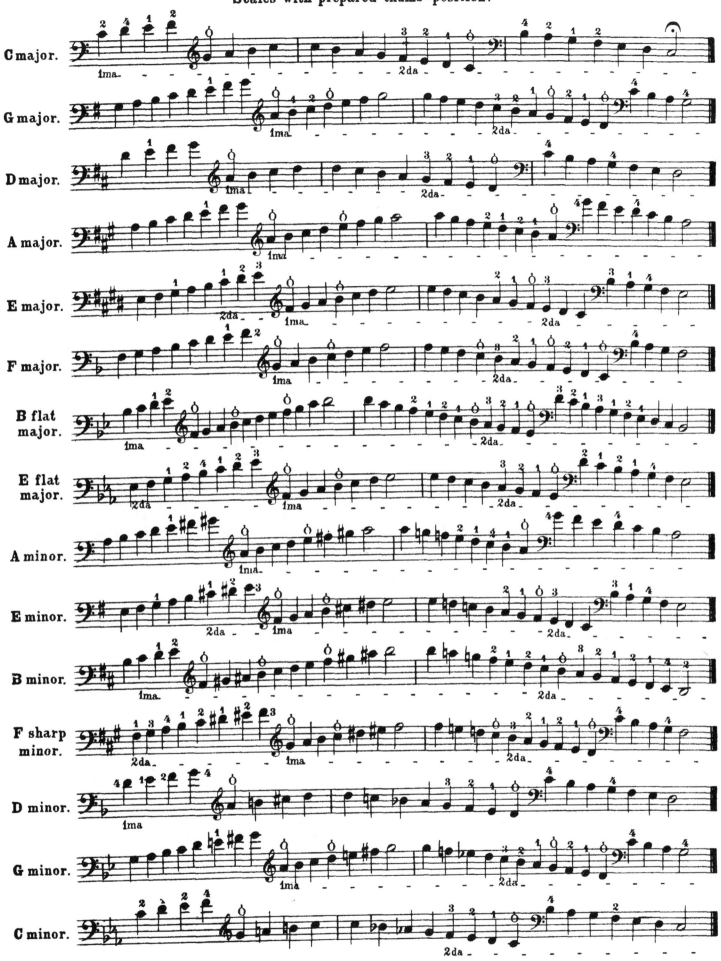

Several scales in the same position of the thumb.

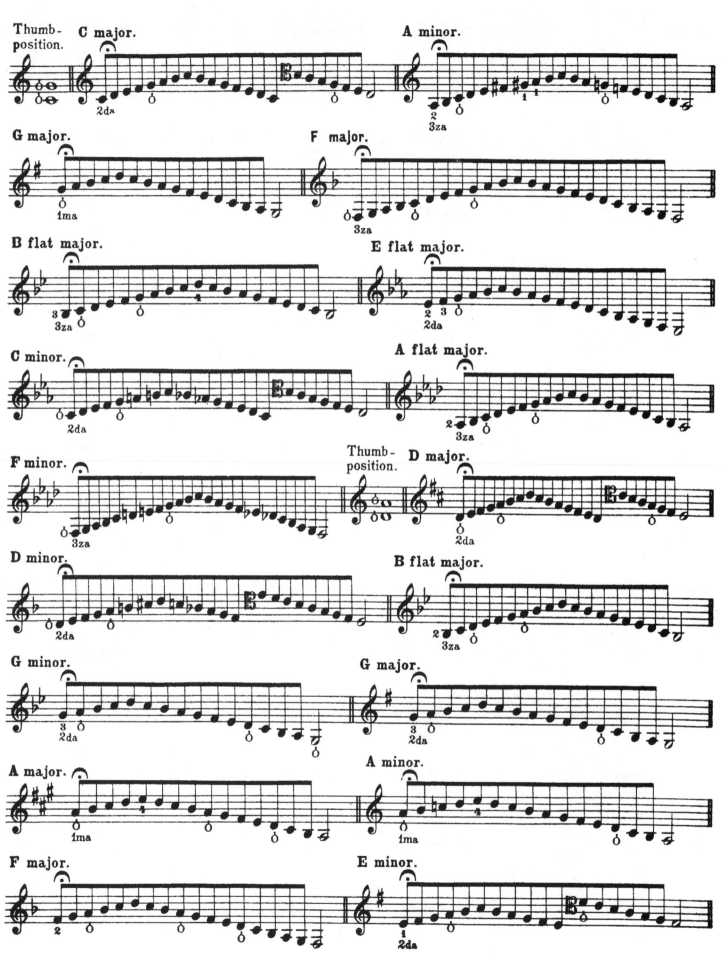

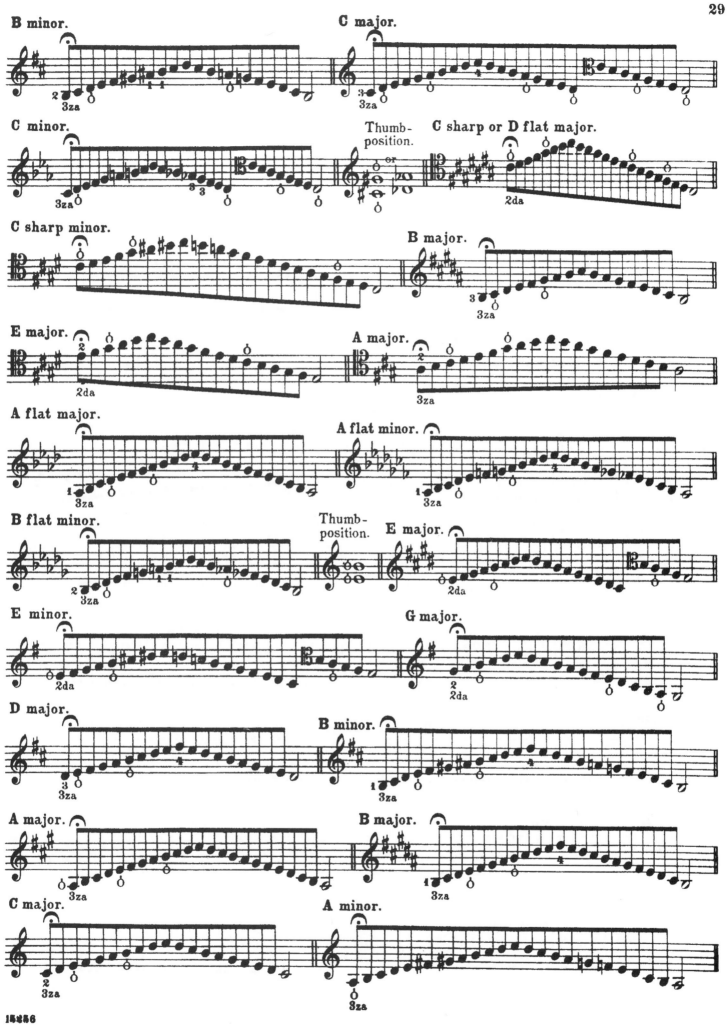

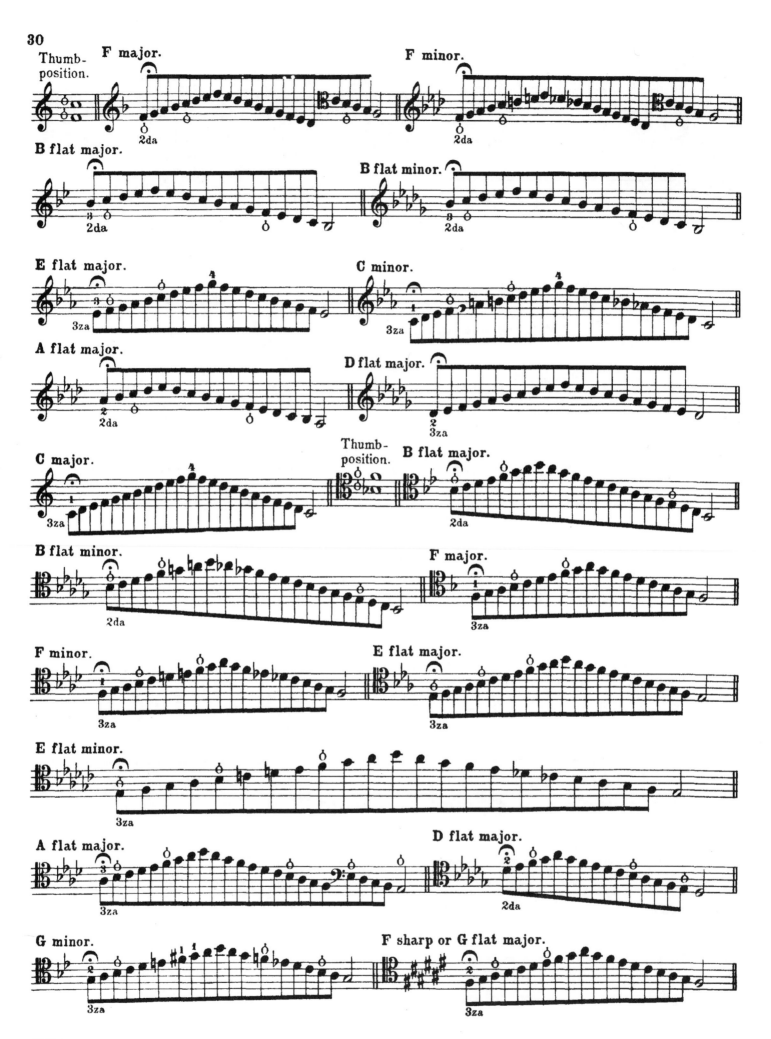

When playing octave-passages in the thumb-position, it is necessary that the student, in order to acquire clearness and perfect intonation, should never lift the 3rd finger, when moving the thumb along, but should always move it along with the thumb.

The hand then remains as quiet as possible; only the distance between the two fingers just mentioned gets smaller and smaller in ascending passages; in descending ones the distance naturally increases in the same proportion; for instance:

Exercise in Octave-passages.

Variations of the above.

Here the turning of the bow must be effected by the right wrist.

In order to enable the pupil to practise the Octave-Exercises also on the D- and G-strings, let him imagine them to be in the bass clef with a ♭ for signature; in measure 11, a ♮ instead of the ♯, and a ♭ instead of the ♮.

The rules for octaves apply for thirds and sixths; yet passages in these do not occur so often in violoncello-music.

Trills and Double Trills in the thumb-position.

Longer Exercises for the thumb-position will be found in the Appendix, Nos. 102 to 107, and Nos. 109 to 112, incl.

15. Harmonics.

Harmonics are produced if the strings are not as usual pressed firmly down upon the finger-board but only lightly touched with the fingers. They are exceedingly pleasant to the ear, on account of their bright, bell-like tone. However, harmonics cannot be produced at any desired point of the string; many also differ not only in sound, but in degree, from the notes produced at certain points by firm pressure (in the ordinary way). It is a normal rule, that, if the exact centre of a string be lightly touched with a finger, the note produced, when sounding the string with the bow, is the higher octave of the tone of the open string.

On the A-string we thus have ....

If now we move the finger a little higher up, towards the bridge, and thus shorten the string to one-third of its length, we obtain the fifth above the octave, viz: ....

A quarter of the length of the string gives the double octave ....

the fifth part gives the third above this double octave ....

the sixth part the fifth ....

the eighth part the triple octave ....

These are the harmonics mostly in use. They are found at those points of the string where the same notes would be obtained, if the strings were pressed down firmly upon the finger-board.

But harmonics are also found if, instead of moving the finger from the centre of the string *upwards* towards the bridge, we move it in a similar way *downwards* towards the nut. The following drawing will afford better information on this subject, than lengthy explanations, which really belong to the science of acoustics.—

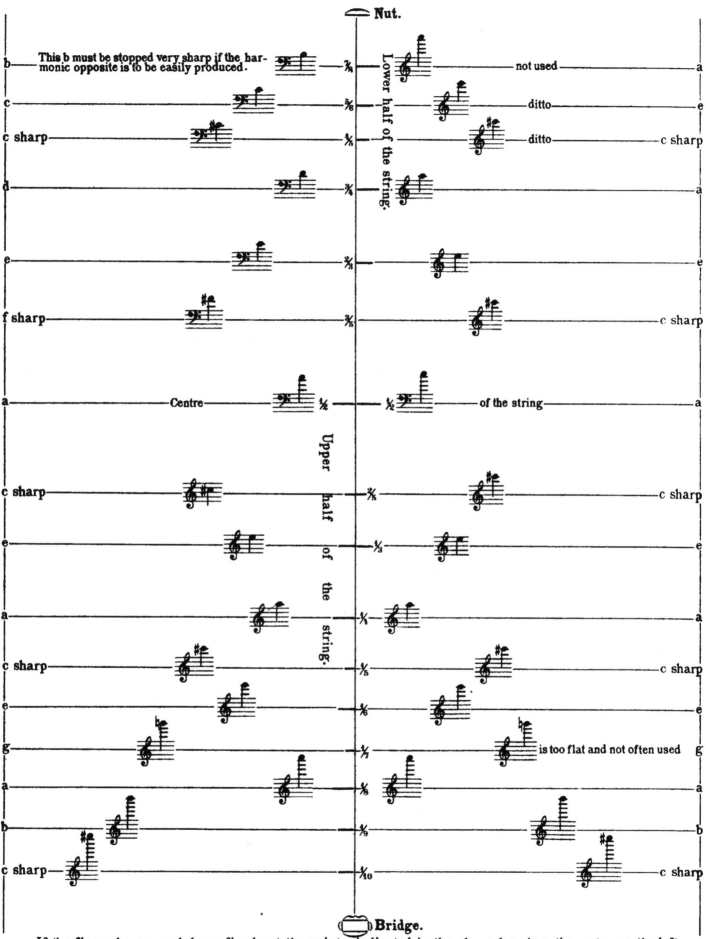

Nut.

This b must be stopped very sharp if the har-
monic opposite is to be easily produced.

Lower half of the string.

not used — a

ditto — e

ditto — c sharp

Upper half of the string.

Centre ½ — ½ of the string — a

is too flat and not often used

Bridge.

If the finger be pressed down firmly at the points indicated in the above drawing, the notes on the left are obtained; if it be laid only lightly upon the string, the harmonics on the right are produced.

Harmonics in the upper position.

NB. The notes we enclose with a ⁝⁝ do not sound as readily as the others, and are, therefore, not very often used. Those marked * must be taken firmly, otherwise they sound an octave higher, as the small notes show.

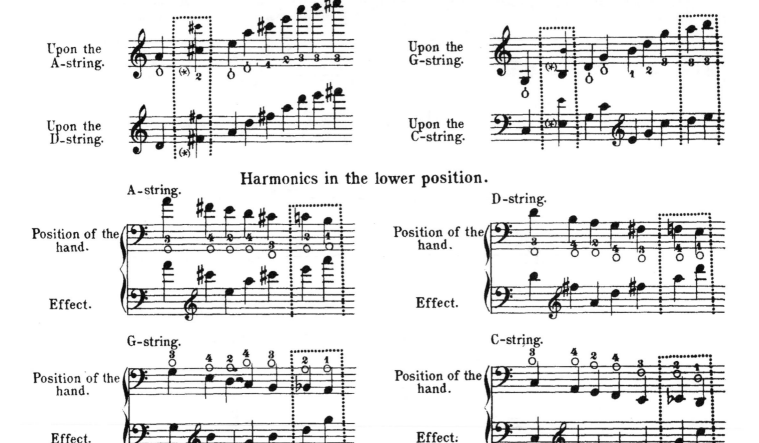

Harmonics in the lower position.

Besides these two kinds of *natural* harmonics, a third kind can be *artificically* produced by using the thumb-position; the thumb is placed firmly upon the string, and the fourth upper note is lightly touched with the third finger.

In this way, *artifical* harmonics are obtained, which form the double octave above the note stopped by the thumb; for instance:

On each of the other strings, of course, the same harmonics are produced a fifth lower.

Harmonics are marked, like the open string, by the sign ○, above which the finger is written which is used for their production (see the example before the last).

Exercise № 108 of the Appendix belongs to this Chapter.

16. Pizzicato.

The word *pizzicato* means, that the notes which are thus marked are not to be played with the bow, but plucked with one of the fingers of the right hand (the 1st or 2d finger). Whilst doing this, the thumb forms a sort of rest for the hand, leaning against the side of the fingerboard where the neck of the instrument joins the body. The strings must never be pulled so vigorously that they strike the fingerboard. A double-stop is executed by the 1st and 2d fingers; a chord of three notes, by the thumb, first and second fingers; if, however, the Chord contains four notes, the thumb may strike either all 4 notes by itself, or only the 2 lower ones, while the 1st and 2d fingers play the 2 upper ones. — In rapid pizzicato passages it is advisable to take two or even three fingers. To do this properly, however, considerable practice is required.

Exercises for the *pizzicato* are in the second violoncello-part of Nos. 69, 76, 85, 89, 93, 99 and 104 of the Appendix.

17. On Tone and Execution.

It should always be one of the pupil's principal aims in practising, to acquire a sonorous and powerful tone. Of course he is fortunate, if the possession of a good instrument having a clear and full tone and answering readily to the bow on all notes, favors him in the attainment of this object. But if he relies solely on this accidental advantage, thinking that it will obviate the necessity of careful study to obtain a good tone, and that by mere physical force he will, after all, be able to produce the power and fullness required, he will be easily surpassed by others, less favored with regard to the quality of the instrument, but knowing how to manage the latter more skilfully and correctly. A full and rich tone is not obtain by excessive exertion, but by judicious distribution of strength.

The fingers of the left hand add greatly to this, if they are at all times set firmly upon the strings, in order to allow them the necessary freedom for vibration. Placing them upon the strings negligently and languidly, hinders free vibration and produces a dull and subdued tone.

For the rest, the tone depends exclusively on the skilful management of the bow; and the force to be applied in bowing should réside in and result from a free sweep of the bow, rather than heavy pressure on the string.

The bowing must also be done in as straight a line as possible, i. e., care should be taken, that the hair remains exactly on that point of the string where it began the note, to the very end of the bow; it never should move up or down towards bridge or fingerboard. — The student, for this reason, should take care that the point of the bow be never raised nor lowered more than is exactly necessary, according to the Chapter on guiding the Bow (page 4).

The most suitable place for drawing the bow across the string is about two inches from the bridge, and this is equally suitable for brilliant passages, and for sustained notes requiring a sonorous tone. It is left to the player's judgment, in passages of great softness, to play a little nearer the finger-board, and in those that require stronger emphasis, to play nearer the bridge. He will naturally be mainly guided by his own observations on the individual condition of his instrument.

If the student, while bestowing attention upon perfect intonation and strict time, follows the way we have indicated, with time and diligence he will become an accomplished player. The violoncello offers many advantages as compared with other instruments. On account of its beautiful tone it is, before all others, adapted to touch the soul and the heart of the listener, if only it be played with true feeling. A few notes on it are sometimes far more effective than many elaborate passages; the player should, therefore, avoid all overcrowding of graces &c.; — they certainly can change the form of a composition, they perhaps embellish it, but they can never breathe life into it. Let the pupil remember that the highest aim of the virtuoso's skill is to breathe life and soul into the body which the composer has fashioned of tones.

The power to attain these results is a matter of artistic temperament, an emotional product which is purest and noblest when it springs from natural and unaffected simplicity.

But as we are neither in possession of means to measure the imagination, nor of expressions to determine the different sentimental faculties of the mind, we are unable to give sufficient theoretical rules on the subject. We must therefore look for models, which incite and cultivate these our mental faculties: as such we may take all artists who know how to give warmth, sentiment and life to their productions.

With regard to the *crescendo* and *decrescendo*, the very basis for the execution of the *cantilena*, we may take a good singer as principal model, and imitate him on the instrument; or the pupil may follow the example of a good instrumentalist. On paper these different fine lights and shades can, of course, be expressed but imperfectly; for instance:

Sometimes a player can lend more brilliancy and expression to a tone by a certain oscillation, produced by placing the finger firmly upon the string, and letting the hand make a tremulous motion; in order to be able to do this with more freedom, the thumb is laid quite loosely on the neck of the instrument. This oscillation, or "close trill", as it is sometimes called, is marked by the sign ⁓ ; for instance:

(Exercises on the *cantilena*, are Nos. 72 to 85 of the Appendix.)

We would, however, warn the pupil, not to let this practice become a fixed habit, and the leading style of his playing. He must never unlearn the art, to be able to draw with sharper outlines.

Let him also take heed, not to change the tempo too often, i. e. not to hurry or retard in certain passages; this would unavoidably lead to a morbid stade of constant wavering. Only a reasonable and judicious use of this grace, to represent increased passion, will agreeably stimulate the fancy of the listeners.

The gradual sliding up or down of the finger, from one note to the other, in intervals of thirds, fourths, &c., certainly produces an agreeable effect at times; but we must again warn the pupil to abstain from the continual, or even frequent, use of this grace. Ear and feeling run the risk of being so completely spoiled by these habits, that after a time even the greatest exaggerations in these graces seem tasteful to the player; while any ear that is not so spoiled would be as unpleasantly affected by them, as by continual moaning and wailing.

The habit of trying to indicate expressive passages by affectedly rocking head and body to and fro, is equally reprehensible. Expression can be produced only by correct shading of the tones, never by affected motions; it is through the ear, not the eye of the listener that his feelings are to be acted upon by the artist. In rapid or difficult passages, the greatest possible physical repose is an advantage, which the learner should acquire. However much the multitude may imagine, that the player is executing something extraordinary only when he visibly makes violent efforts, the true artist and connoisseur know very well, that it is an essential quality of an accomplished player, never to let the listener perceive that one passage is more difficult than another.

We have still to mention:

(1) The Springing Bow (*spiccato*). This bowing must be practised in the middle of the bow, with the forearm and wrist. Hold the bow between the 1st finger and thumb, the 3rd finger resting lightly on the nut and aiding but little in holding the bow; the other fingers touch the stick very lightly. Take long strokes at first, without letting the bow spring; gradually, after the movement has been well studied, and somewhat more hair is used, the bow will spring by itself. Take care not to carry out the stroke with the wrist alone, as this styly of bowing has no strength and produces a poor tone. Begin practice on the open D-string, as it is

the most convenient.  Begin slowly, and increase the tempo to presto.

Good preliminary exercises are to be found in No 8, page 13. The Study given in the Appendix must be thoroughly mastered in slow tempo before venturing on a more rapid movement.

(2) The Tremolo. Is produced solely by the wrist-motion, and as swiftly as possible. It often occurs in orchestral parts, and is indicated thus:

The stronger the tremolo required, the nearer to the nut should the bow be carried.

Major Scales in Four Octaves.

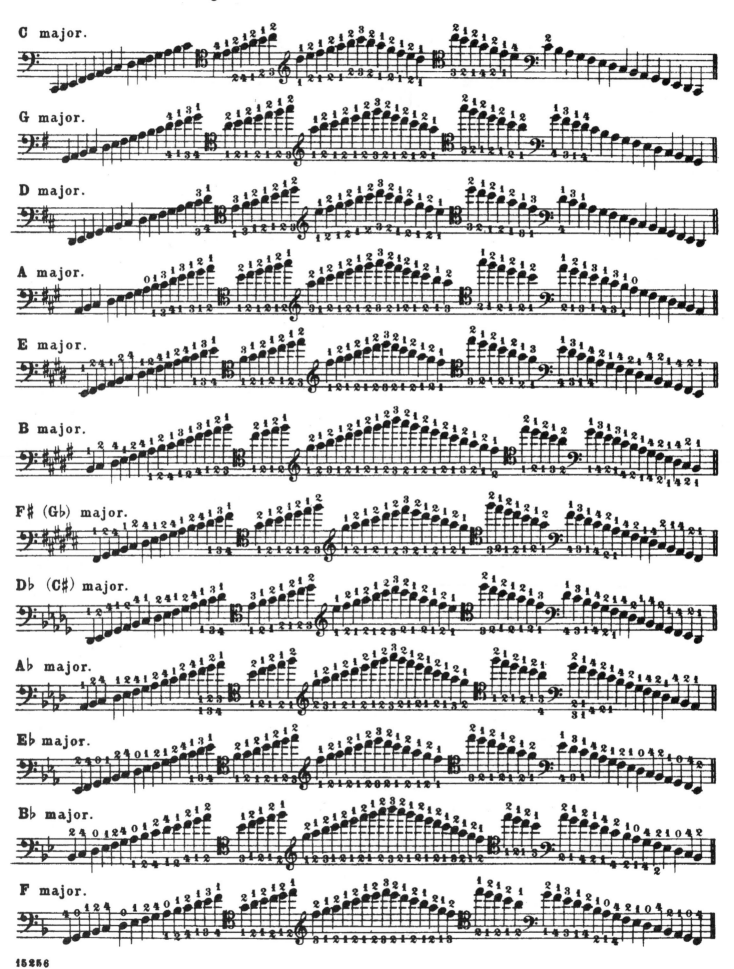

Minor Scales in Four Octaves.

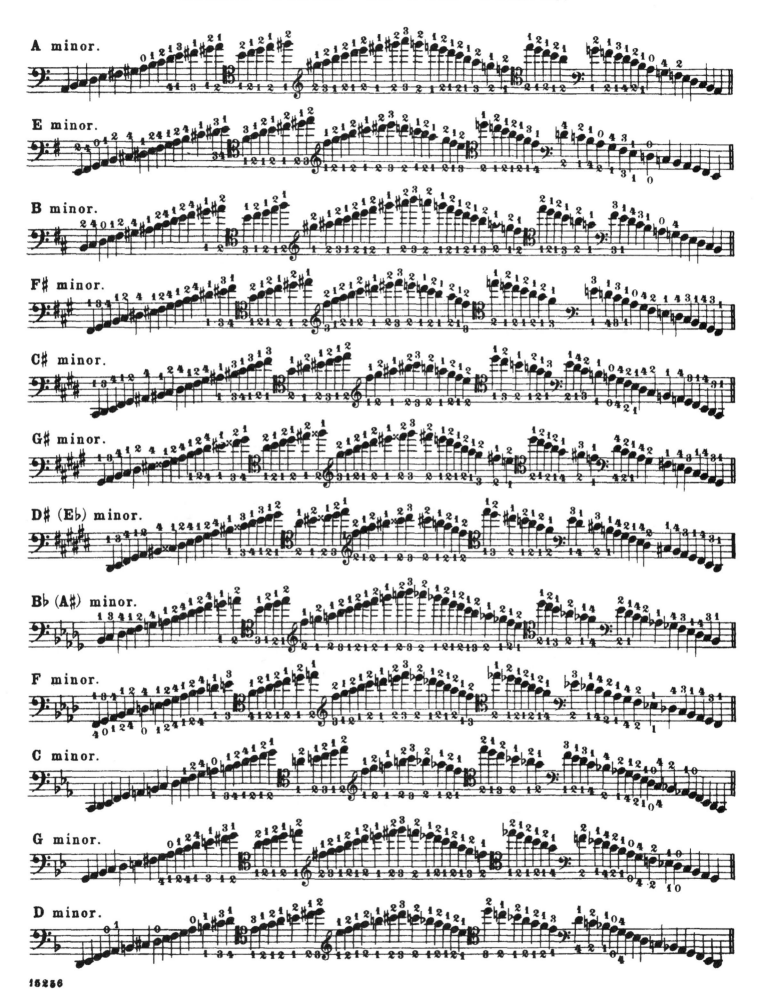

APPENDIX.
Exercises for the Open Strings.

All the exercises must be played with a full, pure tone.

Exercises in the Positions.

41

15256

15.

16.

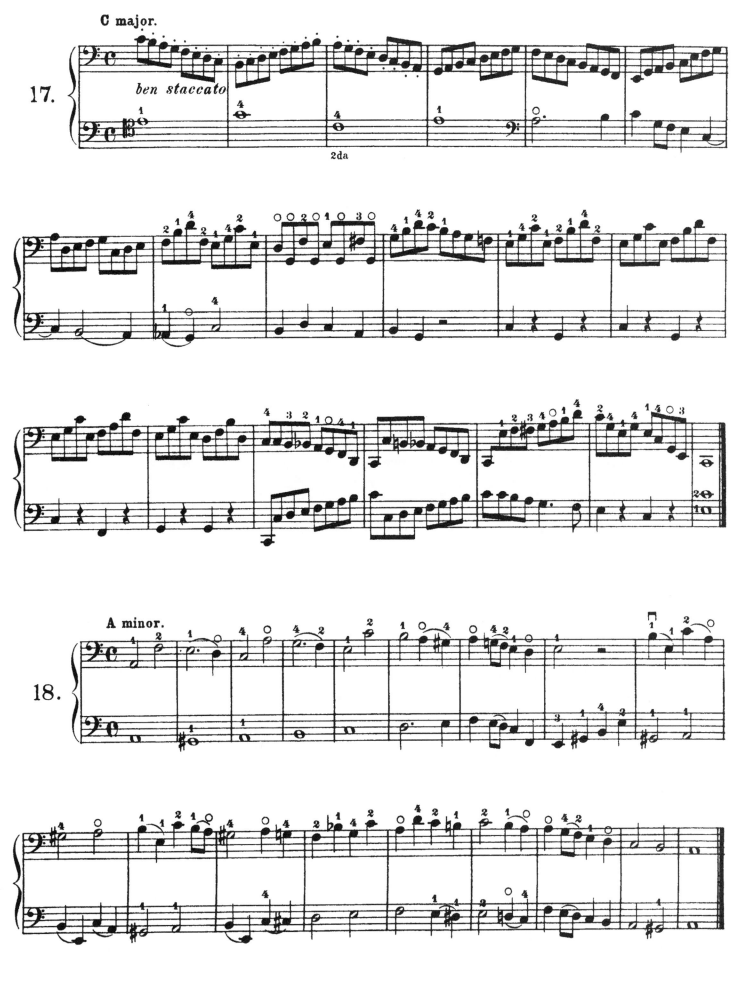

Positions.

24. *p ben legato*

25. D major.

B minor.

27.

Molto moderato.

28.

A major.

29.

30.

34.

C♯ minor.

F major.
Allegro.

35.

42.

43.

C major.

leggiero

Exercises for the right wrist.

Different Bowings to 44.

G minor.
Allegro.

47.

p leggiero

48.

F major.
Allegro.

49.

Different of Bowings to 49.

Allegro non troppo.

50.

Bowing - Exercises.

53.

G major.

ben staccato

54.

55.

57.

D major.
Molto moderato.

58.

legato

59.

60. A major.

2da

61.

Different Bowings to 61.

62. B major.

2da

63. F major.

3za

2da

Different Bowings to 63.

1.   2.

legato

68.

G minor.

Different Bowing to 68.

1.

2.

legato

Different Bow-
ing to 69.

C major.
Allegro.

71. Different Bowing.

pizz.

arco

pizz.

2da

Exercises in Style.

72.

Cantabile lagrimoso.

73.

Cantabile languido.

74.

Cantabile languido.

82.

Exercises in Chromatic Passages.

Arpeggio.

88.

Arpeggios on three Strings.

Different Bowing to 89.

Arpeggios on four Strings.

90.

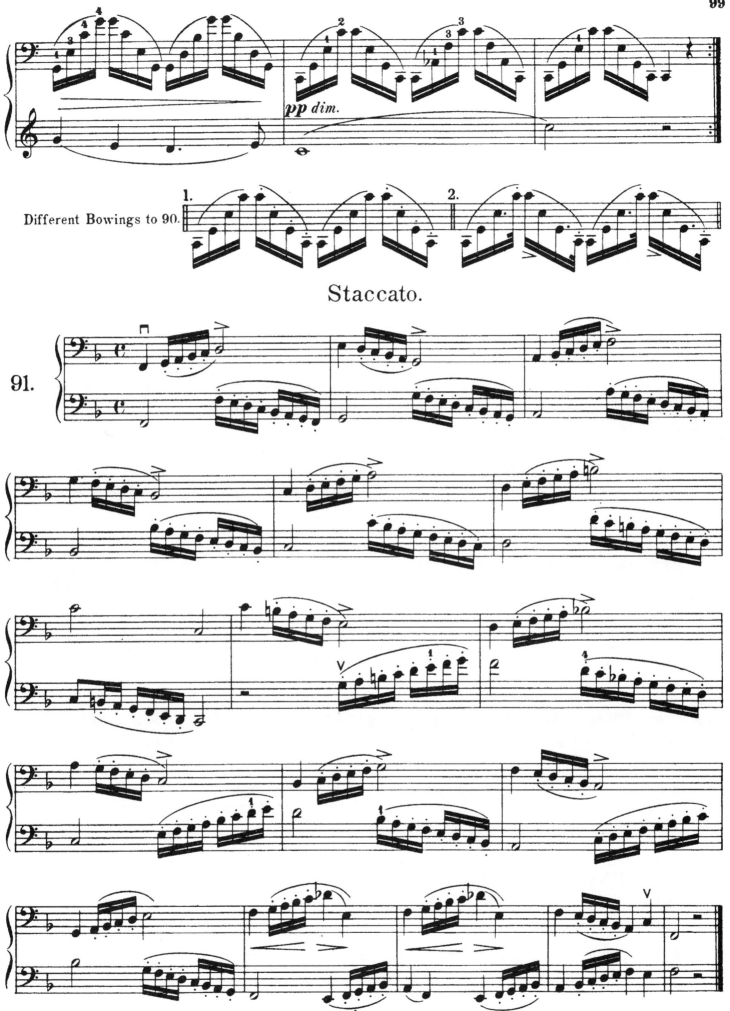

Different Bowings to 90.

Staccato.

91.

Exercise on the Staccato.

The Turn.

93.

*) To be executed

The Passing Trill.

Maestoso.

The Thumb-position.

Harmonics.

sounds:

108.

Study on Octaves.

Tempo ad libitum.

109.

segue legato

cresc.

Study on Thirds and Sixths.

111.

Moto perpetuo.

PAGANINI. [L.S]

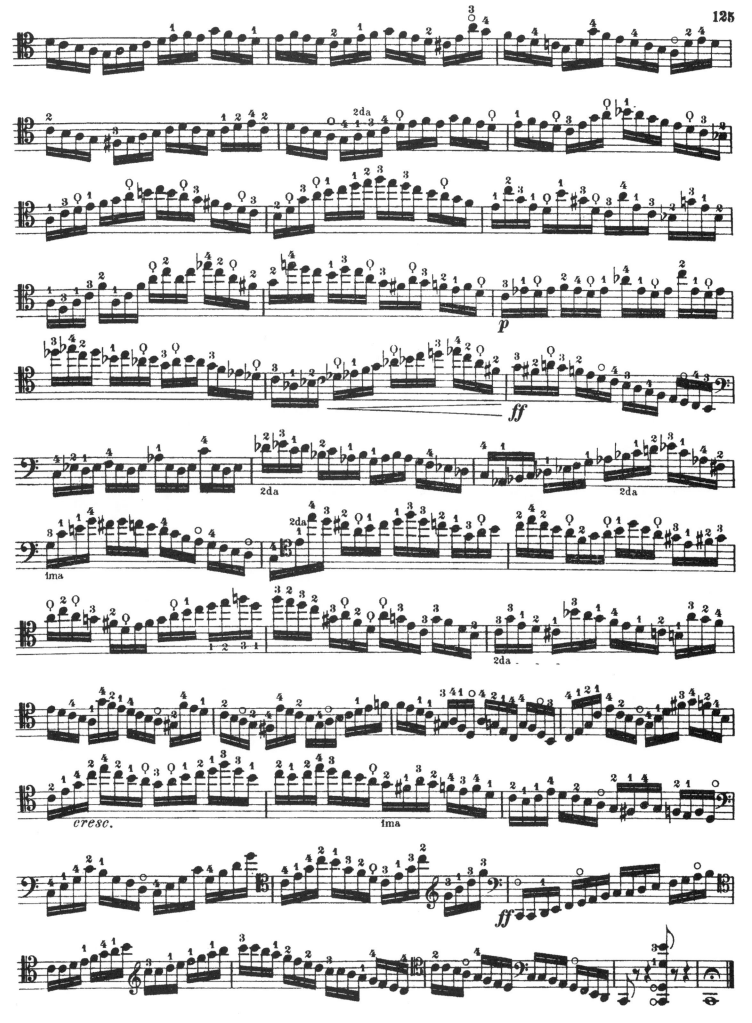